UCLA Star

This Songwriting Journal
belongs to

Stella Keating

If found, return to

Candia NH Stella Keating 595

north , mom- 682-5193

I Am Your Songwriting Journal

By Danny Tieger

P PETER PAUPER PRESS, INC.
WHITE PLAINS, NEW YORK

OUR COMPANY

In 1928, at the age of twenty-two, Peter Beilenson began printing books on a small press in the basement of his parents' home in Larchmont, New York. Peter—and later, his wife, Edna—sought to create fine books that sold at "prices even a pauper could afford."

Today, still family owned and operated, Peter Pauper Press continues to honor our founders' legacy—and our customers' expectations—of beauty, quality, and value.

Illustrations by David Cole Wheeler
Additional images used under license from Shutterstock.com
Designed by Heather Zschock
Copyright © 2015 Peter Pauper Press, Inc.
202 Mamaroneck Avenue
White Plains, NY 10601
All rights reserved
ISBN 978-1-4413-1886-2
Printed in China
7 6 5 4 3 2

Visit us at peterpauper.com

I Am Your
Songwriting
Journal

Contents

Introduction

Hi, I'm your new Songwriting Journal.

You can call me Journal or Notebook or Diary or some name that I don't even know yet, like Bob. You can call me anything you want, just put it on my nametag . . .

HELLO
my name is:
Stella

. . . unless I'm a library book and if I am, try not to write on my pages! Instead, you can use a bunch of loose pages or the back of a school notebook (because let's be honest, no one ever fills those things up).

If I am your book, WRITE ALL OVER MY PAGES! Just read them first.

I am here with one job and that job is to teach you how to turn your amazing ideas into mind-blowing songs! How do I know that you have amazing ideas? I can tell from the way you opened me up. You were looking for something, something to change this boring afternoon into an exciting one. Or maybe to change this exciting afternoon into a crazy one!

Or maybe it's morning, in which case I'm going back to bed. **PLEASE let me sleep for 5 more minutes!**

No matter what time it is, you opened me up looking for something AWESOME and guess what? You found it. And so did I!

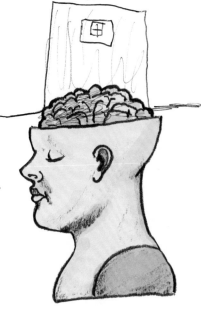

All of the AWESOME that you are going to find in this book is actually in your head right now. And that's because you already know everything you need to write an amazing song! It's all crammed into that mushy part between your ears. I'm going to help you put it onto these pages. I mean your ideas! Not your actual brain.

That would be so gross.

(If this picture is too gross, just add a hat.)

Why should you write songs? That's a very good question for you to answer for yourself.

Some people write songs because they are SO happy that just talking about their feelings isn't enough.

Or sometimes a person is too sad to say how they feel and singing about it is easier.

No matter if they're happy or sad, people write songs to share stories. Songwriters share stories like grandmothers share freshly baked cookies:

ALL THE TIME!

Oh, that gives me an idea! You should take a break and go eat a cookie, you know, for your brain! Maybe you can have a second one for me.

Take your time.
I'll wait here.

Still here.

I'm sure you could guess that songwriters snack all the time. Did that cookie make you feel like a real songwriter? No, not yet? You will soon. After all, you are very smart! In fact, you are the smartest person reading this book right now.

Trust me. I've been read by tons of people.
You're the smartest.

However, being smart or clever is only part of being a songwriter. Songwriters have "Rules" that they follow to help them create their music, "Rules" to help their songs sound better, and "Rules" to keep them structured.

I'm going to help you learn some of the "Rules" for songwriting. I'm also going to put the word "Rules" in quotations because "Rules" is a word that often means not staying up, not eating candy, or not climbing a wall on the side of a restaurant. "Rules" usually have a whole bunch of "NOT" in them, but my "Rules" don't! My "Rules" are more like Tricks. OH! Maybe I should just call them Tricks! I'll have to go back and cross this paragraph out later. Oh, but that reminds me of my first Trick!

If I forget to cross out the paragraph
above, you can do it for me.

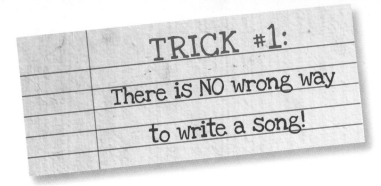

TRICK #1:

There is NO wrong way to write a song!

But there is a RIGHT way to begin! Start with the part that inspires you first! For example, maybe you have been humming a little tune in your head for a couple days that you've never heard before. Or, maybe a few words have been bouncing around your brain and they keep making their way into your schoolwork. Or, maybe you have something to say to a close friend and you're looking for the right way to do it.

Each of those ways of starting can lead to a truly awesome song. And since there is no wrong way to write a **Song**, I've decided there's also no wrong way to read a book about songwriting. So here are some shortcuts that might get you writing songs sooner.

If you play an instrument and you've already begun writing songs, you might want to start reading this book at the Music Chapter on page 67.

If you're not that interested in playing music BUT you still want to write songs, that's totally fine! There are tons of songwriters that don't play instruments. They're called **Lyricists** and if you're going to be a lyricist you might want to start with the Words Chapter on page 45.

Then again, If you wanna learn everything there is to know about song-writing you can read this book in order and start with the Ideas Chapter on page 23.

OH! One last super-important thing before you keep reading: If at any point, if you suddenly get inspired to go write a song, don't wait! Just flip to any blank page and start writing!

Ever after

It sarted when I was asleep um um um but then I heard a little beep beep um um um and I know you don't like me but that was just once and you should love me now cus I do to ya I do to um um um sooooo ever affter ever affter[1] I know that it's hard right now but your to strong right now to move along ever affter[2] It stared when I was aslepp but then I herd a little beep ~~beep beep~~ beep.

Thanks for waching

well, it was.

11

TRICK #2:
Save your ideas!

When you're writing the words to your songs and you want to change them, don't erase them; just draw a clean cross-out line through the stuff you want to skip. The words you crossed out might not work in that song, but they might turn into a whole new song tomorrow. Also, that means your pages will tend to get a little messy and I think most great things start with a mess!

(Or end in one!)

I'm going to teach you lots of Tricks to songwriting! Tricks to help you collect, catalogue, and edit your ideas. You see, songwriting can be hard, but it's not magic. Magic is making a dove appear out of a hat in front of an audience while wearing a sparkly jacket. You won't need a sparkly jacket to write songs, but you're welcome to wear one. And where will we have all of this fun? On my beautiful blank pages! It just so happens that I have left tons of space for your great ideas.

Go ahead, flip through!
Oh, that tickles like crazy!

Somewhere in this Journal you might start writing a song you'll finish 10 years from now when you're a Famous Rock Star touring the world. Hold on to all of your ideas so you can share the best ones!

Here's a blank page for ideas, words, or drawings that might someday be in a song.

I like the way you talk
I like the way you walk
mabe we will have a
love story so I'll ~~beg~~
your pardon, I'll give
you a pice of cease
I'll say sorry and I'll
say please what ever
could we do to
somewon like you
this is just the
start of ~~something~~
~~new~~ new gril frend²
I'll beg your pardon
I'll give youa
pice of cease I'll
say sorry and I'll
say please what
could I do to
somewon lik you

13

Ladla||Ladla
I was standing right
next to youyooo and
I thot you were
my love, and I relised
that I should not
of stepall in frount
of you soo baby
you now what I
mean, so don't talk
to me, You'l be ok,
cause you are strog

and brave, so don't break it, you'l never be along, you'l alwas's be in my hands, you'l never step foot away from me, ood yay I'll be right there soo don't get me ron, no matter what we ~~douwwl~~ alwas's

This one has a dinosaur in a bathtub.

stik togerter like gle,

15

There's almost as much open space in this book as there is written space. That's not by accident! Because I figured if I was too full of MY ideas, there wouldn't be enough room for YOUR ideas, and you'd be stuck scribbling in margins like people do in other books I know. The margins might be fine for a science textbook, but not here! Here your ideas are the star of the show.

In fact there's even a pocket in the back to keep any extra ideas that happen outside of my pages. You can use it for photos, secret notes, or even your chewed gum (but you'll probably only get to use it that way once).

Now, some people might be afraid of a journal like me. They might feel intimidated to start writing because they're not sure their ideas are good enough to write down. This might give them a case of **WRITER'S BLOCK**. Writer's Block is the feeling like you've suddenly lost all of your good ideas. And all creative people bump up against that feeling from time to time.

Some of the terms in this book, like "Writer's Block," have different definitions, so I put a bunch of them in the Glossary in the back (on page 151). You can choose the definition that works best for you. Whenever you see a word in red boldface like **this**, it's in the Glossary.

> There are lots of different ways to get past writer's block. My usual way is to **Doodle**. I, your Songwriting Journal, am full of doodles: some that I've completed and others I've left for you to finish. I think doodling is a great way to get your creative engine running. Try it in the space on the next page.

Draw an alien doing
something crazy,
like this:

Now turn these shapes into different pictures or doodle something around them.

(You can save some of these for the next time you're stuck . . . if there even is a next time.)

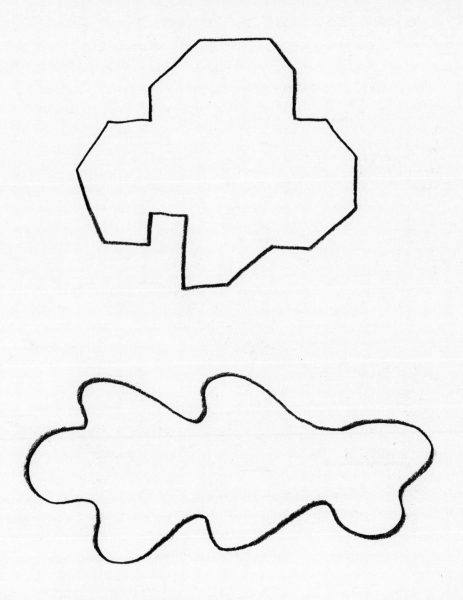

Doodling is the third thing I like to do with a pen. (The first is to write songs and the second is to pretend the pen is a moustache.)

19

Oh, I feel so much better now that you're not afraid to write on my pages! Now let's talk about what songwriting actually is. I think that:

Songwriting is using interesting words and interesting music to share interesting ideas.

Hmmm. While that definition is okay, I think it could be a lot better. I need the help of a **Thesaurus**! You know Thesaurus. She's that helpful book that is always suggesting other words to use. She hangs out all the time with **Dictionary** and **Rhyming Dictionary**. I'll bet you didn't know that the three of them are in a band together called "Twisted Linguistic."

Let me try that again with Thesaurus's help. How about this:

Songwriting is using captivating words with enchanting music to share spellbinding ideas!

That sounds like it's describing a big song from a musical. But that's only one kind of song. I bet I could change the words to sound like a popular song from the radio. Here goes:

Songwriting is using explosive words with robot music to share futuristic ideas!

Or:

Songwriting is using dangerous words with exciting music to share revolutionary ideas!

The more that I think about it, the more I don't think there's just one answer. I left an example for you to fill in, or you can leave it blank and come back to it after you've written your first song.

Songwriting is using _____exciting_____ words

with _____revolutionary_____ music to

share _____dangerous_____ ideas!

The bottom line is, songwriting is using words and music to share ideas! And it's your job to figure out the right combination for your new song! Which one should you start with? The right one, of course. And guess what? There is no wrong way!

21

This page is mostly blank,
except for that octopus
eating ice cream.

I's your brithday, soo

eat a cakes that

your mom will make,

and then celerbrat!

I's goar brithday!

happy brithday to

you, are you 1,2,3,

4,5,6,7, if your

let's celerbrat

Ideas Chapter

This chapter is all about coming up with amazing ideas.

Your ideas are amazing and writing them in songs will only make them better. Songs can take a simple idea and make it larger than life. Or they can take very complicated ideas and make them understandable. The biggest and ultimately most helpful idea you can come up with in songwriting is the reason you're writing your song.

TRICK #3:
Write a Song for a reason!

You ask: Why?

Great question! So great that it gets its own Trick number!

TRICK #4:
Ask WHY?!

Asking **WHY** is the best way to figure out the reasons for things. "Why" is a question that doesn't have a wrong answer. It only has right answers, as many as you can think of!

"Why" does all that? Why yes it does! Why ask why? Why do songs need reasons? They don't always, but if you can figure out the reason you're writing something, it gets much easier to write. **A reason gives your songwriting direction, which is like having a destination.**

AND YOU ASK: Why do you need a destination? Well, imagine walking out your front door and NOT knowing where you were headed. You would make a left turn for no reason, make a right turn just to be even, and probably end up a little lost. **It's easy to feel lost if you don't know where you're headed.** Knowing where you are going helps you make some big decisions about what directions to take.

Here's a songwriting example!

Let's say you are going to write a love song. The **REASON** might be to make someone fall in love with you! That's a tall order to fill in only three minutes, so you're going to need to choose your words and music carefully. You might try writing lovely music and beautiful lyrics. You might try describing him or her as a playful otter or a handsome trout. You might even reveal how you *really* feel. The point is, knowing **WHY** you were writing helped make decisions about **WHAT** you needed to write. (If you think singing about love is gross, TOO BAD! The truth is, love is used a lot in songwriting because when people grow up they spend a lot of time looking for love. That and the best pizza in town.)

The line "It's easy to feel lost if you don't know where you are headed" would make a great title for a country song. Maybe you should write it.

25

Here's a list of reasons why you might write a song.
I left a few blank for you to fill in as you go.

List of Reasons for Writing a Song:

1. To start a conversation

2. To tell a story

3. To share a secret

4. To remember something forever

5.

6. To describe a feeling

7.

8.

9. To complain about a hardship (like chores)

10. To draw attention to an injustice in the world

11. To talk about your bling (sparkly jewelry)

12.

13. To make someone fall in love with you

14. To be silly

15. To celebrate a person, place, or thing

16.

17.

18. *To practice your rhyming skills*

19.

20.

21.

22.

23.

24.

25. *To show off how great you are at making lists*

If you have to memorize something for school, writing the information into a song is a great way to remember it. For example, the song "**50 Nifty United States**" makes it super easy to remember every state in alphabetical order.

> *Looking for an awesome birthday present for a friend? Why not write a flattering song about them?*

Then again, this trick can get you into trouble. You might think you can't start writing without a BIG reason. But that's not true and it brings us to our next trick:

TRICK #5:
Just start writing!

Don't just stare at an empty page waiting for a great idea to come along. You may just need a little patience to get your ideas flowing. So just start writing and trust that you're going to figure it out as you go. It's like leaving your house and wandering around your neighborhood for a bit until you remember, "WAIT, I want a double fudge chocolate milkshake!" and then you'll know just where you're headed.

(If you do go for milkshakes later, feel free to "accidentally" spill some of it on this page. I love chocolate sauce, or at least I think I would, if I could eat anything. CURSE MY LACK OF A MOUTH!)

Let's **JUST START WRITING** now. Pick one of the shapes on the next page and fill it in with writing until no more words will fit. If you get Writer's Block and start feeling stuck, ask WHY? Maybe you can describe feeling stuck to help you get unstuck. Or doodle around the shapes.

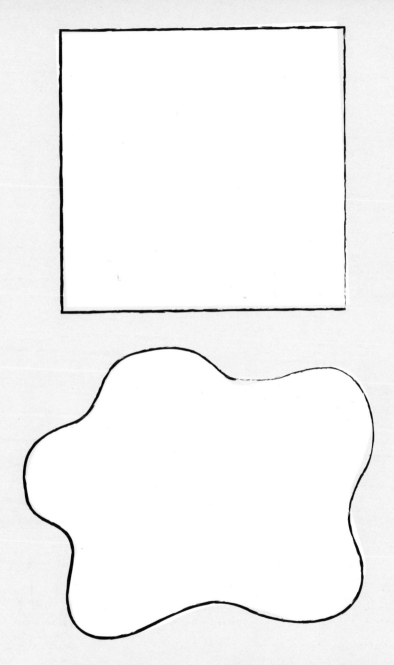

Great start, you're on a roll!

If you are still feeling stuck and not even doodling helps, here are a few other ways to cure Writer's Block:

1. Listen to a song you wish you had written. ✓

2. Start by writing the last line of a song and then write the rest backwards.

3. Jump on your bed. ✓

4. Jump on someone else's bed, then straighten the blankets so they'll never know.

5. Go for a walk.

6. Call someone you haven't spoken to in a while.

7. Learn a new dance. ✓

8. Imagine the perfect Saturday. ✓

9. Argue with your sister or brother.

10. Wish you didn't have Writer's Block.

11. Do your homework.

I'll bet Number 11 cured it.

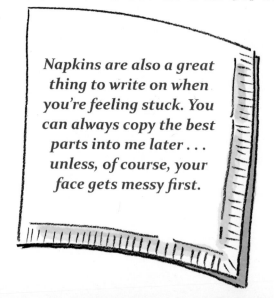

Napkins are also a great thing to write on when you're feeling stuck. You can always copy the best parts into me later . . . unless, of course, your face gets messy first.

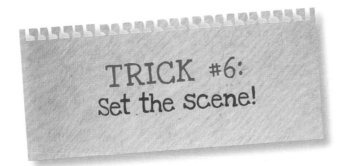

TRICK #6:
Set the scene!

Some incredible songs were started with songwriters feeling lost and writing about their feelings anyway. Let's start working on a song using what you have around you right now.

Stop reading for 10 seconds and really look around the room. I'll count for you. 1, 2, 3, 4, 5, 6, 7, 8, 9, 10. Then play the Observation Game on the next page.

You never know what object you see,
or what simple little piece of writing
might end up in your songs.

Observation Game

Imagine you are an adventurous archaeologist and you've just discovered an ancient location: the room you are in. It hasn't been seen by anyone in over 1,000 years. You'll need to present your discovery to a museum when you get back home, so use the handy space below to make notes about this extraordinary place in complete sentences or short phrases.

What does it look like? pink, my room, Small, dog, and cupcake.

What does it sound like? tik tok

How does it make you feel? happy

WHY?! I love it

Here is some space to draw something from your location:

Now look at what you've written. First find anything you wrote that says exactly where you are and cross it out. For example, maybe you're at school and you wrote, "I'm in my classroom." Now circle the phrases that *really* describe this mystery place, such as "The sound of pencils scratching," or "The slowly moving clock." Pick three or four of these phrases.

1.

2.

3.

4.

Looks like you just started your first verse, which is one of the parts of a song. There are **Verses**, the **Chorus**, and the **Bridge**. First, let's look at the difference between the Verse and the Chorus. The Verse of a song is typically where you describe the details of your story: Where you are, what you're doing, and maybe even how you got there. The Chorus is where you talk about how the story has changed you. In other words . . .

You will find Observation Song fill-in pages in the back (pages 90–91) that help you catalogue your answers from this exercise into a song.

TRICK #7:

The Verses are the story and the Chorus is how you feel about it.

This is one of my favorite Tricks—it is especially true in country music. Here's one example of this Trick. I started writing a song about Cinderella, with a short version of her story in the Verses and a Chorus about how it makes her feel.

Cinderella Song

VERSE 1:

Once upon a time there was a sad little girl
She lived with an evil stepmother
She was forced to do all the chores
And never felt like anyone would love her.

VERSE 2:

She asked to go to the palace ball
But her stepmom just said, "NEVER!"
Then her fairy godmother appeared
And changed her luck forever.

CHORUS:

She was finally loved by someone after feeling so alone.
She was finally loved by someone and the love was all her own.

VERSE 3:

When she got to the ball she saw him
And the prince was staring too
After just one dance she fell in love.
And everybody knew.

CHORUS:

She was finally loved by someone after feeling so alone.
She was finally loved by someone and the love was all her own.

BRIDGE:

How would she treat her wicked family
They had proved they were unworthy of?
Would she scorn? Would she banish?
Would she warn? Would she punish?
No she chose to show them love.

CHORUS

They were finally loved by someone after feeling so alone.
They were finally loved by someone and the love was all their own.

I like how the Chorus stays (almost) the same even though we're talking about a few different kinds of love: the motherly love of her fairy godmother, the romantic love of a prince, or forgiveness for Cinderella's stepmother and sisters.

To get started on your first song, use your answers to the Observation Game on pages 32–33, you know—where you were writing about your place as if you were discovering it for the first time, like an archaeologist. If you need more inspiration, do something you've never done in that room before. Like 37 jumping jacks or maybe a two-minute headstand. One time I got put away on a shelf upside down and did a headstand for two weeks! I'm awesome!

Here's an Imagination Game to get you inspired:

Adventure Game

While minding your business one afternoon, a strange woman in a blue cloak gives you a mysterious map. Follow the map and write an Adventure Song about the incredible places it takes you. OR write a song about the journey itself.

I can't wait to read your **Adventure Song**, imaginary or real! Check out the fill-in Adventure Song pages in the back (pages 96–97) to help you with your song.

Listening Assignment:

Spend some time listening to oldies, songs SO good they've lasted for more than 50 years of radio play. Pay attention to the first few lines of songs. My guess is the singer is sitting by a bay, waiting in a station, or on a highway. Or maybe a combination of all three.

Songs are also a great place to share your ideas about the world. People like Woody Guthrie wrote hundreds of songs about the way the world worked, and sometimes didn't work. You may decide that your songs are going to have a message too. If so . . .

TRICK #8:
Put your message in the Chorus!

The Chorus tells how you feel about the story in your song. So the Chorus is the message.

Have you ever heard the song, "This Land Is Your Land" by Woody Guthrie? I bet you have. It's a fun song to sing because it's mostly just a list of beautiful places that Woody thinks belong to everyone. He even goes trespassing in the song to prove that point. Right there in the title is the message he's sharing, and you repeat it for him every time you sing the Chorus. His mission becomes his message. No matter what reason you choose to write a song, put that big idea right in the Chorus so that you say it a lot!

Some people call this part of the song the **Hook**, which doesn't have anything to do with *Peter Pan* except that in both cases the Hook is the part that will catch you. Songwriters call it being "catchy," which means it will get caught in your head. If you're wondering what your message might be, I have a Trick for that! See Trick #11—Write what is true for You!

TRICK #9:
The Bridge takes us somewhere else.

The Bridge transports a song to the next part of the story. It can be about you reaching a new level of feeling or it can literally be about you moving to a new place. In each example the Bridge changes something. Here's a few examples:

Bridge about running away.

I feel stuck.

I feel better and think I'll stay.

Bridge about discovering cheese.

My sandwich is the best.

Maybe it can be better.

Bridge about finally sharing feelings.

She doesn't notice me.

A new chance at love.

Typically a Bridge happens a little over halfway through a song and has the highest, most intense singing in it. Your Bridge is a great place to ask some big questions or even address some part of your story that you haven't found space for in your verses. For instance, in the Cinderella Bridge, we get to find out what happens to her family and learn JUST how wonderful Cinderella is.

The biggest difference between the Bridges in songs and the bridges over rivers is that there are no trolls hiding in songs. And there are probably THOUSANDS of trolls hiding under bridges. I mean, I'm guessing that's true, since I'm a *talking* book.

While you're out there adventuring you might consider bringing your backpack or a writer's bindle (a handkerchief or cloth in which your important stuff is kept, attached to a stick). That makes it easy to master the next Trick . . .

TRICK #10:
Bring me on your adventures!

This Trick has two meanings.

1. You should bring ME (or another notebook) with you when you go on adventures because inspiration can strike at any time.

2. Your song should take your listener on an adventure using details. Many songs start their adventures by describing the setting in the opening line.

TRICK #11:
Write what is true for You!

Try writing about something that you are an expert on: something that you can sing about with authority. Maybe you have a special recipe for the best sandwich in the world or you know what cats are actually thinking. Maybe you have an opinion on how people should treat one another or you have a secret worth telling. The point is to start with something YOU believe, so it's easy to get excited to write about it. There are fill-in pages in the back for writing a **Mission Message Song** (pages 102–103).

Future Song List of Inspiring Things

1. What makes your best friend the BEST friend.

2. *her happiness*

3. *her laughter*

4. *her smile*

5. DNA (Deoxyribonucleic Acid)

6. The right amount of cheese on a cheeseburger.

7.

8.

9. How eyes work.

10.

11.

12.

13.

14.

15. The difference between ice dancing and figure skating.

You may have just put something on that list that someone else has already written about. Do you think that's going to be a problem? NOPE.

TRICK #12:
"Good writers borrow and great writers steal."

This trick is borrowed from . . . well actually it's a funny story. People have credited this quote, or something like it, to everyone from Pablo Picasso to Igor Stravinsky. In reality, someone named W. H. Davenport Adams originally wrote it in an article in which he was complaining about bad poets. So what does it mean? What's the difference between borrowing and stealing?

Here's what I think:

When you borrow an idea you have to say where you got it from, which is fine, but it always stays the other person's idea. You have to give them credit and write their name in the back of whatever it is you made. However, when a writer "steals" an idea, they take the part that matters most to them. And when they sit down to use it, they must change it to make it fit their new purpose. The process of modifying that idea changes it into a new idea! Then it's yours and someone else can steal it from you!

So really, it's truer to say that good writers borrow and great writers are constantly being inspired by other's work. But I think "steal" sounds better.

I also think it's time to get to the nuts and bolts of songwriting. It's time to talk about music and words.

Thankfully that's just ahead in the next two chapters! But before we go, here's some space for a list of things you're going to steal from other people's songs. Once you become a famous songwriter you may want to destroy this page so you don't get found out.

Sneaky List of Stolen Ideas:

1. A Chorus that says, "You are *beautiful beautiful*"

2.

3.

4.

5.

6.

7.

8.

9.

10.

11. A part of the song that just goes "ooooh ooooh ooooh."

12.

13.

14. A Bridge that says, "I'm going to change, I promise."

15.

16.

17.

18.

19.

20.

Ideas Chapter Notes

You can use this space for anything you want.

Or you can rip it out and spit your gum in it, which would be a great way to get rid of your sneaky list of stolen ideas.

Words Chapter

This chapter is all about coming up with the right words.

I LOVE WORDS!

What do I love even more?
YOUR words! And this chapter
is all about them.

This chapter is all about what words you are going to sing. It has a bunch of Tricks to help you figure out the perfect words to describe a feeling, experience, or person in your songs. After all, unlike real life, you'll have time to think about what you're going to say and craft it to perfection.

Ah, words—arguably the greatest invention in the history of human beings. Words are extremely powerful and sometimes hard to speel. Uh, spell. (Remind me to fix that later.)

STOP! If you decide your song is not going to need words, just call it an "instrumental." Instrumentals are very popular at loud desert festivals and on quiet elevators.

There are lots of different kinds of words, like Nouns, Verbs, and Adjectives. There are lots of different ways to use words, most commonly we are told to use them in Complete Sentences.

Have you checked out any of the definitions in the Glossary in the back? Go ahead and look now, I'll keep your place. It starts on page 151.

I'm sure your teachers have told you that you need to write in complete sentences. That's when there's a subject, like a noun, plus a verb. Now don't get me wrong, sentences are great! In fact, there are a ton of them in this book. Like that last one. However, the best part about writing the words for songs is that they don't have to be grammatically correct. In other words YOU DON'T NEED TO WRITE IN COMPLETE SENTENCES because you are writing Lyrics. Lyrics are what we call the words in songs, and it brings us to our next Trick:

TRICK #13:
Write the thought, not the sentence!

This is great news! It means you can use fewer of those bothersome little words otherwise junking up your beautiful lines and write only what you need to. Lyrics do not have to be written in complete sentences, because they are poetry. And poetry has no "Rules"! Just go read the poetry that Allen Ginsberg wrote. It looks more like this:

> "Whole families
> shopping at night! Aisles full of husbands! Wives
> in the avocados, babies in the tomatoes!"
> —from *A Supermarket in California*

The way people think thoughts, not the way they normally get written down.

Most of Ginsberg's poetry is written for adults but some of it is weird enough for kids to enjoy.

To be honest, some poetry, such as sonnets, has a ton of those "Rules." A sonnet has to have a certain number of lines, with a certain kind of rhyming, and even a certain number of syllables in each line. Trouble is, I certainly don't remember any of those rules. SO . . . I guess you don't have to learn them either. The only poetry rules we're going to discuss are **Rhyming** and **Rhyme Scheme**.

People love rhymes! Why? Because they make words feel like they fit together, like they were meant for each other. Let me show you what I mean:

So much time of everyone's day,

Is trying to think of the right things to say.

When a rhyme comes along in a wonderful song,

And you felt it was coming from the melody you're humming,

It all fits together,

Much better than a real conversation.

It might have the same information,

But there's far more . . . elation.

The outcome is simply a different effect,

Cause rhyming means words go together perfect.

I know! I know! I should have written the word as "perfectly," but I didn't have to because I'm writing lyrics! Plus I'll do anything for a rhyme!

Listening assignment:

Spend the next few days listening carefully to your friends and family and count the number of accidental rhymes they say in a day. Oh! There's one. *I'll bet there will be more than you're expecting.*

RHYMES

So in less lyrical terms: Rhyming is fun! It is fun for the listener, fun for the singer, and fun for the writer. Let's practice rhyming with **Rhyming Couplets**. A couplet just means "two lines" and you already know what rhyming means. Use any word to finish the couplet below—just make sure it rhymes with "mat."

In front of my door is a welcome mat,

And sitting on it is a purring

You could write "bat," "hat," "rat," or "fat" . . . but the words "sitting" and "purring" probably made you think of a "cat."

Now replace the whole second line with whatever you want, just make sure that last word still rhymes with "mat."

In front of my door is a welcome mat,

.

That time you could have used any rhyme at all because without "sitting" and "purring" there wasn't the same context. *Context* is just a fancy word that means, "The details around the thing you're talking about."

Finish a few more rhyming couplets and try writing your own.

He flapped his wings and flew into the sky,

....

....

They all lived happily ever after,

....

....

education,

....

fire station.

....

orange,

....

door hinge.

....

....

....

....

....

....

....

....

You finished those rhyming couplets, now finish these pictures. Or leave them for the next time you have Writer's Block.

Now, writing couplets is a good place to start, but it gets trickier when you're writing more than just two lines at a time. That's why we have something called a **Rhyme Scheme**. A rhyme scheme is a repeating pattern of rhymes that lasts for several lines. It gets repeated the same way in each Verse and then switched around a little bit for the Chorus. How do we keep track? Read on.

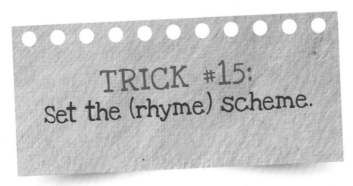

TRICK #15:
Set the (rhyme) scheme.

People write rhyme schemes as AABB, ABAB, ABCB, or something wackier like ABCDEE. This just means that each letter stands for a line that ends with a certain rhyme sound. "A" lines sound the same and "B" lines sound the same. Here's an example:

AABB

This is a simple start,	A
To an important part,	A
It's couplets that rhyme,	B
Two lines at a time.	B

Or ABCB

This is a little easier,	A
Cause not all of them count,	B
The first and third are only there,	C
To make the right amount.	B

You can also think about ABCB as one LONG AA rhyming couplet:

AA

This is a little easier cause not all of them count.   A
The first and third are only there to make the right amount.   A

I'm sure right now you're thinking, "Hey! You said you were going to make this easier! This is complicated."

You're totally right, but with a little practice I'm sure you'll pick it up. Just remember to make sure the A lines end with the same-sounding words and the B lines end with the same-sounding words.

Here's a topic to write about: The Forest!

	A
	A
	B
	B

Now write about your favorite dessert.

	A
	A
	B
	B

TRICK #16:
Check your rhymes out loud.

It's always a good idea to read your lyrics out loud to make sure they rhyme. Sometimes words that look like they rhyme actually sound different, like "love" and "move."

How about you write about your breakfast!

	A
	B
	C
	B

ABCB is a pretty great rhyme scheme because the A and C lines don't have to rhyme with anything. They're just there to help make your B lines better.

Here's a crazy one! Write about your teacher!

	A
	B
	A
	B
	C
	C

Rhyme schemes will help you compose your rhymes but you don't need to start with them! I think it's much easier to start writing based on your ideas or words, and plan the rhyme scheme later. That way you are free to follow your great ideas without worrying whether or not they rhyme the right way. You might discover that ABAB is going to work a lot better than AABB. Remember to work with a rhyme scheme that helps your song, not just one that is complicated . . . which brings us to our next Trick.

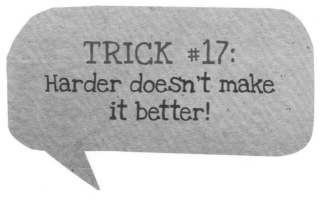

TRICK #17:
Harder doesn't make it better!

The truth is that sometimes no matter what you try, you can't find the perfect rhyme. In those dire situations you might need the help of a **Half-Rhyme**. A half-rhyme is two words that almost sound the same. Like:

"Time" and "Line"
"This" and "Assist"
"Club" and "Love"

and

and

BEWARE!

The half-rhyme is a hungry half-rhyme, half-beast creature that roams the countryside looking for freshly baked pies cooling on windowsills and howling at the moon at night!

TRICK #18:
Sing it like it rhymes.

It's the oldest trick in the book! Just change the way that you sing a word. Hold the "ahhh" a little longer or swallow the "ist" sound at the end. You are in control of the way your lyrics sound since you are the one singing them! For example,

Loving youuuuuuu

IS Troubuuuuuuuuuuuu(le)

Or

My day is totally open

Seeing you is what I am hopin(g)

Still can't find the right rhyme? You have two options. The first option is to simply not rhyme and adjust your rhyme scheme later. The second is to . . .

TRICK #19:
Invent a new word!

The technical term for this is "coining" a word or a phrase. It's as simple as using an old word in a new way or combining two words in a way that hasn't been done before. And who knows? If you create an amazing new word, it could become a full-fledged part of your language . . . unless your language is French. (The French are particular about what is French enough to be French.)

> **WARNING:** You should never claim that a fake rhyme is a real rhyme. But you should also never let someone else claim that one is better than the other.

The master of word creating was writer William Shakespeare. He wrote plays, poems, and songs in the early 1600s. Shakespeare invented words like "lonely," "hurry," "generous," "eventful," and "bump." Oh, and like over 1,000 more. Do you know what the biggest difference between YOU and William Shakespeare is? He was bald. See? And there's no reason you need to wait until you're bald to come up with some new words. If you are bald, you must already be as cool as Shakespeare.

Here is some space to start your collection of coined words. (I came up with a couple too.)

1. **Glozy**, *adjective: GLOW-zee. The shine on your face when you are feeling extra cozy.*

2. **Somnabulurking**, *adjective: som-NA-bu-lurk-ing. That feeling you get when a dream follows you into your waking life.*

3. I was walking thout he

4. forist when I met a prince he was so

5. hansome and he gave me a kiss,

6. know I know that love comes slow

7. oooooo ya love comes slow, I was

8. walking throu the forst when I met

9. a prince he was so hansome and He

10. gave me a kiss, now I know love comes

11. Slow Salmon ow
    ow ew oo ya love
12. comes slow ~~water~~

13.

14.

15.

16.

17.

Now that you have several new words to use in
your songs, I've got to share an awesome way to
use them! Send me your new words and I'll post
them on our "New Words" web page on
www.iamyoursongwritingjournal.com,
so other kids can use your words in their
songs. Remember to include the definition and
pronunciation.

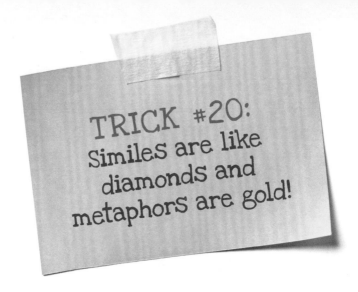

TRICK #20:
Similes are like
diamonds and
metaphors are gold!

Similes and **Metaphors** are the technical writing terms for ways of comparing two things. Similes use "LIKE" or "AS" in the middle of the two things. Metaphors just say that one thing "IS" the other thing. (Use the title of this Trick to help you remember!) This might feel like a tiny difference and it is, unless you're trying to write the perfect lyric. Let me show you the difference in a few lyrics.

Simile: My friend is LIKE a rock.

This lyric might mean that your friend is strong and dependable.

Metaphor: My friend IS a rock.

*This lyric might mean that your friend can be
thick-headed and immovable.*

Literal: My friend is a rock.

*This lyric might mean that you have a best friend
who is actually a lump of brainless stone.*

See how it can make a pretty big difference? Also, you may not want to sing the second option to your friend, unless of course they are an actual rock, which would be pretty weird.

Here's some space to write a simile
about your best friend:

My best friend is LIKE a

_____

_____

Here's some space to write a metaphor
about your best friend:

My best friend IS a

_____

_____

Now see if you can use a metaphor or a simile and the rhyme scheme below to write a poem about someone you know. If you can't think of a person to write about, make someone up!

To ....

.... A

.... B

.... C

.... B

.... D

.... D

I wrote a poem about you on the opposite page. If you have read everything up to this point, you are probably ready to write some amazing poetry with some awesome ideas. BUT... I Am Your Songwriting Journal and that means it's time to make some magnificent music!

A Poem to YOU

You are great at reading out
loud or in your head,

In your living room or
sitting in your bed.

You are great at writing like
Shakespeare but with hair,

The songs that you are dreaming
up are wonderful to share.

Your head is full of ideas; your
hands are fast to write them,

And if a puppy saw your songs,
they would try to bite them.

Keep them safe, keep them sound,

And keep your Journal close around.

Words Chapter Notes

Music Chapter

This chapter is all about coming
up with the perfect music.

I am tempted to say that the best way to learn music for songwriting is to have a friend or family member teach you a few chords on the guitar or keyboard. You'll struggle a bit but after a ton of practice you'll be rocking those chords so hard you'll have to go learn more. This is how lots of songwriters start. However, that would make this chapter exceptionally short. So while you're thinking of who to ask to teach you, I'll keep teaching you Tricks for writing music.

What is **Music**? Is it just the sound that instruments make when they're being played right? No. It's so much more than that. The English word "Music" comes from the Greek word *Mousike* which means "like a Muse." In ancient Greece, a Muse was a magical person who was able to inspire others to do or make amazing things. I think that is a pretty great definition of music.

Music, noun. Sounds that inspire amazing things. What things? So many different things!

Music is one of those rare creations that can be different for everyone! Not only do everyone's ears work slightly different, every person who hears music brings their own life experience to it. That changes the music once it enters their heads.

If a picture is worth a thousand words, music is probably worth a million. In 1913, when famous composer and Scrabble player Igor Stravinsky performed his **Symphony** (a composition performed by a full range of musicians and instruments), *The Rite of Spring*, for the first time, the audience was so "moved" by the music they started shouting and fighting in the theater. Stravinsky's music was so powerful it actually started a riot! Remember that when you sit down to write your songs; you will have the power to make grown-ups act like children (not that you would ever fight in a theater).

Stravinsky
(another cool bald guy)

Take a break from reading and go listen to "The Rite of Spring." Be careful that you don't accidentally start a Riot of Spring!

I wish there was enough space in this chapter to help you write a full symphony like Stravinsky did. But there really isn't! So instead, we're going to talk about a very specific kind of music. We're going to talk about **Melody** and **Accompaniment**. A melody is several **Musical Notes** in an order that you either sing or play on an instrument. Accompaniment is a big word for the music underneath the melody. Remember this is just one style of songwriting but it's a very popular kind. Let's start with the melody. Chances are you've seen something like this before.

TWIN-KLE, TWIN-KLE, LIT-TLE STAR, HOW I WON-DER WHAT YOU ARE!

Learning how to read and write music helps a lot of people write songs. BUT there are just as many songwriters who never learn it. Instead those writers hum melodies into recorders for other people to write down. There isn't one way to write a melody, but there is one thing that will always make a melody better, which leads us to the next Trick.

TRICK #21:
Keep it simple.

Simple means that it's easy to remember, easy to sing, and easy to get stuck in everybody else's head! The word "simple" sometimes seems to be negative, as if somehow something is only really great if it's complicated. NOPE! I think simple is clean and powerful. The simplest way to write a simple melody is to tie it to the words in your lyrics. You know I love to doodle. So here's a game I invented called **Melody Lines** to help you write a simple melody.

Start with a short lyric like this:

"The night was growing colder . . ."

Yeah, that'll do. Now pick the most important word in the lyric. I'm going to pick the word "growing" because it has a nice long "Ohhh" sound and because it's a descriptive verb. Now draw a melody line above the lyric that matches the way you think it should be sung, and changes over that important word. Mine would look like this:

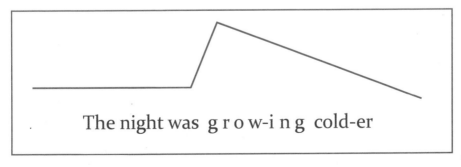

The night was g r o w-i n g cold-er

When you sing this lyric, sing along with your line. The higher the line, the higher you should sing. If you wrote it on a musical staff it would look like this:

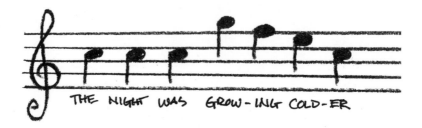

THE NIGHT WAS GROW-ING COLD-ER

Here are some spaces to draw a few more melody lines over the lyrics. Try making two words important in the same line or try breaking up the line into pieces to make the melody **Staccato**. Staccato is a fancy old Italian word that means singing notes separately. Tip: Breaking up the line can be extra helpful when you have a lyric with lots of small words in it:

I had that same old crazy scary sort of feeling

There's a million ways to make me happy

In the city where I was born there was a secret

When you start writing full songs in the back you may want to leave some space above your lyrics to draw melody lines over them. You will also need space to write chords for the accompaniment of an instrument. What kind? Well . . .

TRICK #22:
Pick an instrument that sings to YOU!

HEY!

Every instrument has a different voice, just like every person. You'll need to find one that sounds right to you. You need an instrument that will make you want to play it. However, be warned: Getting the right instrument means that it will sit in your room and shout, "PLAY WITH ME!" until you do. They can be as noisy and as stubborn as Songwriting Journals!

You might choose to play the **Keyboard** or piano! Imagine those beautiful keys laid out before you. Your left hand powerfully hammers out low notes while your right hand expertly tickles out a melody with the high notes. You will join the songwriting ranks of Billy Joel, Norah Jones, Ben Folds, and Lady Gaga, just to name a few.

OR...

You might choose to play the **Guitar**! Oh, the guitar, a curvy little wooden box with six strings. Your left hand confidently bouncing between chords while your right hand is playfully strumming the rhythm. You will join the songwriting ranks of Taylor Swift, John Lennon, and Joni Mitchell, just to name even fewer.

Or you might choose . . .

The Clarinet, Accordion, Tuba, French Horn, Bass, Banjo, Wood Block, Mandolin, Cello, Triangle, Drums, Marimba, Harp, Jaw Harp, Harpsichord, Steel Drum, Bagpipes, Air-horn, Theremin, Spoons, Oboe, Piccolo, Trumpet, Viola, Saxophone, Ukulele, Zither, Flugelhorn, Tro, Harmonica, Bugle, Ocarina, Pan Flute, Pitch Pipe, Washboard, Trombone, Shakuhachi, Didgeridoo, Slide Whistle, Flute, Fiddle, Dobro, Lap Steel, Saw Blade, Lute, or the Jug! Just to name a whole bunch!

If you are not familiar with any of these songwriters or instruments, you should look them up. They might become your new passion!

Whatever you decide, you're going to need some help getting the right instrument. Start by asking your family and friends. Sometimes people have Keyboards, Guitars, or other instruments hanging around from back when they wrote songs. If you do need to buy a new instrument, please fill out this checklist to make sure you find the right one!

My **instrument** will be . . .

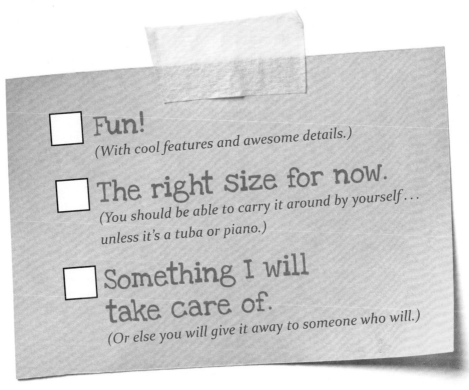

☐ **Fun!**
   (With cool features and awesome details.)

☐ **The right size for now.**
   (You should be able to carry it around by yourself . . . unless it's a tuba or piano.)

☐ **Something I will take care of.**
   (Or else you will give it away to someone who will.)

Nice checkmarks! Looks like you're going to get an instrument. Start by asking your family, stopping to look at yard sales, and even exploring thrift stores. Just like old books, old instruments have lots of stories hidden in them. You may sit down to play it one day and find a whole song ready for you to write down.

If you still can't find what you want, try checking out my website, *www.iamyoursongwritingjournal.com* for deals on some awesome instruments. But first you have to ask a parent, sibling, or teacher! I've pre-written a letter (below) to help. Hopefully we can convince whomever it is you need to convince. Rewrite the letter in your own handwriting, filling in all of the details, and mail it to them so they know you mean business. (If you can't find a stamp, leaving it in their jacket pocket will also mean business.)

Dear _____

(write the name of the person who makes the decisions),

I want to thank you for that amazing Journal that you gave me. It has been so fun learning about songwriting.

I have realized that more than anything I want to play the

_____

(write which instrument)

I promise to play my instrument every day! I promise to take care of it, and I even promise to write you a song about how grateful I am!

Will you please help me buy a

_____

(write in the same instrument as before)

Sincerely,

_____

(write your name)

The letter trick can also work when asking for a new pet. Just remember to change the parts about "playing with" to "feeding" and "caring for."

You might need to wait to get an instrument
but you don't have to wait to start writing songs!
You can write a song right now with
www.iamyoursongwritingjournal.com.

That's right, I know about the Internet! You'll find a bunch of songs at our website that need to be finished and a bunch of song prompts to help you finish them. All of these songs have been especially created so that you can fill them in with your amazing Words and Ideas. If you end up recording them, send them to the website so others can be inspired by your awesome songs.

Once you get that new instrument you can keep reading, but until then remember . . .

TRICK #1:

There is NO wrong way

to write a song!
(see page 10)

Music Chapter Notes

There's more to the music chapter on the next page, but I thought first maybe you'd want to make some notes or finish this picture of a bear fighting a bunch of robots:

You draw the robots!

Hurray! The letter worked and now you have a guitar or a

keyboard or whatever else you were inspired to get! You should probably think of a name for it. Lots of famous songwriters have names for their instruments: B. B. King's guitar is named "Lucille" and Eric Clapton's guitar is named "Brownie." It's a good way to make your instrument, your new songwriting partner, different from any other.

You've probably already started learning how to play your new instrument with the help of an awesome music teacher, a friend, or the Internet. So you probably already know what **Chords** are, how they are three or more musical notes all played together. You might not know just how important chords can be, but they are the first step to accompaniment and they will guide your new melody.

There are tons of different kinds of chords. Chords that sound hopeful are called *major*, chords that sound gloomy are called *minor*, chords that sound like they're questions are called *seventh chords*, and chords that sound unfinished are called *sustained*, just to name a few. There's probably a more technical way to describe chords, but this is how I think of them. And here's how you should use them.

TRICK #23:
Use your music to tell your story!

You need to put your chords in an order that helps move the story along and sounds great! Maybe an Em (or E minor chord) will give your chorus a certain *gravitas*, which is just a great word for being serious. Or maybe you'll end each verse with a seventh chord to prepare your listener for the next part. No matter what chords you use, the order they're in is called a Chord Progression. Let's play one now.

Start by playing the G chord, then switch to the Em chord, then the C chord, and finish with the D chord. Yikes! That looks way more complicated then it is. Let me write it more simply:

G Em C D (repeat)

This chord progression is used in almost every rock'n'roll song from the 1960s. It's just those four chords in that order repeating FOREVER! This is also the chord progression of our Love Song you can listen to on the website *www.iamyoursongwritingjournal.com*.

You can also play it in the key of C. Changing the key of a chord progression is a great way to change the mood of the music you're writing.

C Am F G (repeat)

Or in the key of D:

D Bm G A (repeat)

Now try this new one!

G C G D

Actually it's not new at all. Sounds just like the song "Brown-Eyed Girl" by Van Morrison. Oh, and about 1,000 other songs. Here's a pretty crazy chord progression:

C G Am Em F C Dm G

You might recognize it. The song is called "Pachelbel's Canon." It's by Johann Pachelbel, and lots of people get married to it.

Now it's time for you to make up a Chord Progression. Let's start by just filling in the blanks below with different chords until you find the one you like the best.

1. G Em ___ D

2. G ___ C D

3. G C G ___

4. ___ C G D

Now start from scratch and make up a brand-new one! If it happens to sound like one of the ones you've already done, that's TOTALLY fine.

Write in below some Chord Progressions you like:

Writing songs is all about doing what's been done already in a cool new way with your ideas. This is a lot like the stealing Trick in the Ideas chapter. Copying someone outright is wrong, but taking a musical idea and changing it to fit your new song is what everyone does and has always done. After all, people have been singing and playing music since the dawn of time. Now YOU make up a few progressions:

1. __ __ __ __

2. __ __ __ __ __

3. __ __ __

4. __ __ __ __ __ __ __ __ __

Looks like you might have a Verse progression and Chorus progression in there. Some people will tell you that it's very important to change the chord progression between the Verse and the Chorus, but then again Carly Rae Jepsen's song, "Call Me Maybe," doesn't, and it's a song EVERYBODY loves. However, since the Verse and Chorus are doing such different things in a song it might be a good idea to shake it up. (Not sure what "different things" they're doing? Go back and read the Ideas chapter.)

Here's one way to think about what you're writing...

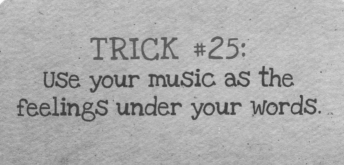

TRICK #25:
USe your music as the
feelings under your words.

Think of how a violin can sound like it's crying or a trumpet can sound like it's laughing. Music has its own voice and when you write songs, your music is going to help you tell the story. It's almost like you have two different "voices" telling the story at the same time. So you want to make sure your music is helping and not distracting from what you're trying to say. One way to totally change the feeling of your progression without changing the chords is to mess with the **Rhythm**.

TRICK #26:
Change the rhythm.
Change the time.

Rhythm is literally the way that time is organized in music. Fast rhythm means there is less time between the beats and slow rhythm means that there is more time between the beats. Try playing your progressions at a slower or faster rhythm to change the feeling.

The same can be true of your words. The speed of your lyrics can convey a lot about the tone. Singing quickly makes you sound excited or nervous and singing slowly can make you sound serious or sad. You could also try changing the rhythm from one part of your song to another. Maybe your Chorus is fast but your Verse is painfully slow. Or maybe your whole song could get faster and faster as you go!

By now you're probably feeling like you have a ton of options every time you sit down to write a song. There are as many ways to write a song as there are things to write about. So, how do you decide which of these options is best for your songs? Well that's easy. The most important Trick for you to remember when you sit down to write your first song or your 45th is . . .

TRICK #27:
You know best!

After all, every one of the Tricks, ideas, and suggestions I've made are only *my* way of doing things. The best person to teach you how to write your songs is going to be YOU!

You'll write one song you love, then three you only like, maybe one that you hate, and then 100 you love again. It's a journey! And speaking of journeys, it's time to get going! So I'm going to stop filling these pages with my ideas so you can fill them with yours. I'll leave a couple of more Tricks open for you to fill in as you discover them. Enjoy the previous chapters if you haven't read them yet . . . and if you have, I am so excited for you to fill this Journal, your house, and your friends' ears with your new songs!

Happy writing!

Your Tricks

TRICK #28:

TRICK #29:

If you come up with new Tricks you'd like to share
with others on *www.iamyoursongwritingjournal.com,*
please email them to:

journal@iamyoursongwritingjournal.com
danny@iamyoursongwritingjournal.com

Songwriting Pages

Pages with fill-in songs and prompts
to help you compose them.

OBSERVATION SONG

Refer back to page 32 if you want.

Verse 1: *Start the story by describing a place in detail. (Use all five senses.)*

....

....

....

....

....

....

Verse 2: *Introduce yourself or whoever else is involved. (Try a metaphor or simile to describe them.)*

....

....

....

....

....

Chorus: *Describe how you/they feel about this place! (Use the same few words a few times so that people can sing along.)*

....

....

....

....

....

Verse 3: *Show everyone where you're going next or if you are staying. (Is there a twist? A surprise detail?)*

....

....

....

....

....

Bridge: *Take us to a new place! (This change can be emotional, physical, or you can literally leave.)*

....

....

....

....

....

Chorus: *Describe how you/they feel about this place! (The last chorus can change a little now that you have changed from crossing your Bridge.)*

....

....

....

....

....

....

I woke up in the m
morning and I was
soo tired, when I
inmired my sister's
backpack, It was
lik I was ~~dreamin~~
dreaming, and then
I saw a light
beaming, I wish
this day woud never
end,

ooo yay and I woke
up the next day
and my dream
was over,

La La Laoo La LaLaLa

It had a dream, about

two houres ~~jumpping~~ Jumpping

over ~~over the~~ the sun, It was

like me jumpping

over a rainbow, whith

a uncorn, a~~nd~~nd then

my mom woke me

~~up~~ up, and It was

all over at school

~~all over~~

I was dreaming

of my family,
and we were
at a chrismas
party, and having
fun together, I
wished this was
realy happning, when
I ~~whent~~ home I
went
dreamed ag~~ian~~in,
and it did,

ADVENTURE SONG

Refer back to page 36 if you want.

Verse 1: *What did you pack in preparation for your adventure?*

....

....

....

....

Chorus: *How do you feel to be out there all alone? Or, if you're with someone, how does it feel to have a partner on your adventure?*

....

....

....

....

Verse 2: *What's the craziest thing you've had to overcome? (Talk about it like it's happening RIGHT NOW.)*

....

....

....

....

Chorus: *Sing about that person or being alone again. It can be the same as your first Chorus.*

....

....

....

....

....

Bridge: *Why are you on this adventure? Why is it important?*

....

....

....

....

....

Chorus: *Same as the last (this time find one word to change if you want).*

....

....

....

....

....

If your heart beats ~~is~~
beating to fast,
give me a call,
and I'll love it
all, and then we'll
go to the mall,
and I'll give you
a ball, and I'll
~~make~~ make you tall,
and I'll make a
wall, and I'll give you

a doll, and I
hope that you
love it all,

You make my heat
happy, you make
bep, bep, bep

I'll be right with you!

Take my hand, don't ever leave
me hanging, baby its all
right, we'll get throw this
together, I'm right here, and
I'll hold you tight, you
have a smile on youre
face, I can see it throw
lips, you're eyes sparle
like the oaeen brease, you
can tell me I'm rong,
but I don't think its
true, I'll be right with you
I'll be standing there, I'll
be right with you baby
I don't care, no matter
what we do I'll be right with,
you you make me shine when
I'm sad you would make me
sad if you ever left I'll
be right with you, I'll be standing
there I'll make you laugh when your sad
Whatever puts a smile on youre face.

101

MISSION MESSAGE SONG

Refer back to page 37 if you want.

Chorus: *What is wrong with the world? And how would you change it?*

....

....

....

....

Verse 1: *A story that describes the problem and a person who's involved.*

....

....

....

....

Chorus: *What is wrong with the world? And how would you change it?*

....

....

....

....

Verse 2: *A different story about the problem with a more hopeful end.*

....

Chorus: *What is wrong with the world? And how would you change it?*

Verse 3: *Your experience with the problem and the reason you wanted to sing.*

Chorus: *What is wrong with the world? And how you're going change it?*

One more night

wait til u see, how many times it might take you to really understand, understand nowon gana say that your dome + stuped nowon's gana drag you down tonight, wo wo wooooo, One more night, til I reach my goal, yeah One more night til beat my scoroe, yeah One more night til t get it all righttt, gana reach my goal, gona beat my score gana get it righttt gona get it, yeah I'm gana get it right, gana get it right soonanof

LOVE SONG

Verse 1: *What was the first thing you noticed about this person? Describe this physical detail and the moment of first seeing them.*

....

....

....

....

....

Chorus: *How does this person make you feel? (Bring up the detail again.)*

....

....

....

....

....

Verse 2: *What is it like to be around this person on a normal day?*

....

....

....

....

....

Chorus: *How does this person make you feel? (Bring up the detail again.)*

....
....
....
....
....

Bridge: *Describe your perfect day with this person and end it by saying how you wish you could really tell them how you feel.*

....
....
....
....

Chorus: *How does this person make you feel? (Bring up the detail again.)*

....
....
....
....
....

Verse 3: *Finish with the first two lines of your first verse.*

....
....
....
....

When we first met

when we first met
I was shy, but you came
along and ~~now~~ now look at
us, oooo When we first met,
It was a love story, I knew
it from the start I looked
in your eyes and I saw
a sweet hansome man ow oo
yah yeah, When we first met
it was a love story, you made
me the happyest girl on eath,
and I love you for that, ooo When
we first met you were
the oneee for me you made
me laugh, you picked me
up, you made me the happye
girl on earth, and I loved you
for that, when we first
met, I looked in his eyes,
and I said OMG I'm
in love, I'm in love, I took y
hand I made it work withou

telling you how the story
begins.

I know you wish I knew wish I had wear you want to be, but I can't read your mind, yeah

I can't read your mind, read your, mind, so give me a break give me a breath, I know your hert, you want to go home, but I know you, yeah I know, you yeah yeahhh I won't hert your, I'll gives it my best shot, your in my arms your not saying a word, saying a word, it's ok if you let me know if your not feeling so well, yeah I know you, know you, I know you very well give me your hand, we'll get throw this together, I'm your frind, I'll lend you a hand, That's just my story begining,)

By: Stella

you you belong with me, I belong with you, nothing gana chang not even the page, that we were on no nothing gana chang not even a thing, nothing gana chang that's were I begin, nothing's gana chang, nothing gana heart you right out of the core cause you belong with me and I belong with you, If we try once we'll be new, If you do that then I will screem If you do this then I will de this If you no I don't like to brag, no, I'll screem loud cause nothing's gana chan not even a thing nothing gana hort you by the heart Roth gana brake you down apart, cause nothing gana you belong with me and

113

SO HARD TO BE YOU SONG/
THE BLUES

Verse 1: *Pretend that when you woke up this morning something was bothering you. Sing about how it bothered you all day.*

Chorus: *Sing that you've got the "thing that bothers you" blues. And there's no way to get rid of it.*

Verse 2: *Sing about how long it's been bothering you and how you've tried to fix this problem in a lot of different ways.*

Chorus: *Sing that you've got the "thing that bothers you" blues. And there's no way to get rid of it.*

Verse 3: *Sing about what's going to happen if you can't stop this thing from bothering you . . . totally over-exaggerate!*

By: Stella Keating

Hard blues

[You were gone, you were out,
I couldn't find you, I looked
around and all I found was
treeees] Somebody found you
brought you any-where] But
then I saw you sitting
on a rock all alone, all
alone, I Repeat picked you up and
I said "It will be allright
Hard blues, every-where, Hard
blues, will look you in thi eye,]
don't look down, or you will
fall to the ground, stay
strong be brave in every-way,"
you were gone, you were strong
we will put our hands togethar,
Hard bules will hit you in
the eye, and screem, you never
saw them come-ing] But
they were there, they were there,
you never saw them com'en and
116 You mean the world to me, I
wana s

Sa-wad-dee-ka

THE DUET

Verse 1: *YOU sing about liking something.*

Verse 2: *YOUR FRIEND sings about really hating the same thing you just sang about.*

Chorus: *YOU BOTH sing about the same thing, using words that don't show how you feel.*

Verse 3: *YOU should keep the same opinion of this thing but hint that you might not always love it.*

Verse 4: *YOUR FRIEND sings about how "hate" is a strong word and that maybe your friend only hates it sometimes.*

....

....

....

Chorus: *YOU BOTH sing the same thing as before.*

....

....

Bridge: *YOU BOTH sing from the other person's point of view at the same time loudly over one another.*

....

....

....

Chorus: *YOU BOTH sing the same thing as before. Only now WE know that you have changed your opinions (a little bit).*

....

....

....

Christmas

gather round the christmas tree, sing some songs that belong in your heart, sing repeat a holiday song, sing a jolly song, on gather round today, break

Christmas oh christmas, Please come to us, we'r standing right here right here christma oh christmas we'r right here singing is the best part of chris but where did christmas goooo where did Christmas goooo Christmas is the best part of the year, and christmas is almost here, I wish I could see all those hearts beat so fast, but where did christmas gooo, yeah where did christmas gooo wish I could open all those preasents on christmasss dayyyy

122

SILLY SONG

Verse 1: *Describe the silliest person you can.*

Chorus: *Explain that YOU are in fact that person.*

Verse 2: *Describe the silliest place.*

Chorus: *Explain that this silly place is your home. (Use as many of the same words from the first chorus as you can.)*

Bridge: *Describe some very serious things.*

Now be awkwardly silent for five seconds . . .

Chorus: *Say you forget what you were saying and then sing the same chorus again.*

CINDERELLA SONG

Refer back to page 34 if you want.

Verse 1

Once upon a time there was a sad little girl
She lived with an evil stepmother
She was forced to do all the chores
And never felt like anyone would love her.

Verse 2

....

....

....

....

Chorus

....

....

....

Verse 3

....

....

....

....

Chorus

....

....

....

Bridge

....

....

....

....

Chorus

....

....

....

I'd love to hear your version
of this song!

Promise

Who ever your with sing a
lala bye, sing a lala bye to
wait for the right Kiss yeah
yeah yeah ah ah ah promises
promices, promises promices mater,
promises, promises, promices, promises
mater, wait just a min. I I I I
lost my voice lost my voice oh oh oh
oh no, promises promises promises
Promises mater

You can run, you can hide, but you can't escape my love, be brave, keep your head up, remeber don't forget, I love you, and that's all I gata do ♥

Glossary

Glossary of Things That You Now Know

Since this is YOUR glossary, it's up to you to circle the most helpful definition, or you can just write your own

Accompaniment
1. The music underneath a melody.
2. The feelings beneath the words.

3. ....

Adjectives
1. Description words.
2. Words some people might use to show how impressive their vocabulary is.

3. ....

Bridge
1. A one-time part of a song that brings your ideas to a new place, like a real bridge.
2. The part of the song where you'll find the highest and most emotional singing.
3. The place where you might find a hungry troll.

4. ....

Chords
1. Three or more musical tones at the same time.
2. The use of harmony to build on the sound of a musical note.

3. ....

Chorus
1. The repeating middle part of a song that shares the song's big idea (and often its title).
2. The part that will get used by other pop songs in famous mash-ups.

3. ....

Complete Sentences
1. A sentence that has a subject and a verb in it.
2. An arrangement of words that conveys an idea or meaning.

3. ....

Dictionary
1. A book filled with most every known word, and their meanings, in a specific language, arranged alphabetically.
2. A living document that grows along with our collective human vocabulary.

3. ....

Doodle
1. Casual drawing done without much thought or revision.

2. ....

3. ....

Guitar
1. A six-stringed instrument many people play in college.
2. A hollow wooden box which resonates with the vibrations of six strings.

3. ....

Half-Rhyme
1. Two words that almost end with the same sound (you'll need to sing them weirdly to make them sound right), like "clam" and "fan" or "love" and "club."
2. Two words that do not sound the same, but people pretend they do to make songwriting easier.

3. ....

Hook
1. That special music phrase that will get stuck in everyone's head.
2. The title or main idea of a song.

3. ....

Keyboard
1. An electric piano that is smaller than a regular piano and easier to move.
2. A tiny computer that plays music.

3. ....

Lyricist
1. The writer of the words in a song.
2. The person standing next to the piano in old-timey movies about writing music.

3. ....

Melody
1. A composition of musical tones in a set order.
2. A short musical "phrase" that tells a story.

3. ....

Melody Lines
1. A fun new game that's sweeping the nation.
2. An easy way to "draw" the melody you're going to sing.

3. ....

Music
1. The sound that instruments make (especially when they're being played right).
2. Something that inspires amazing things.

3. ....

Musical Note
1. A single musical tone.
2. When you scribble a message to someone and then they sing it out loud.

3. ....

Noun
1. A person, place, or thing.
2. A place, thing, or person.

3. ....

Rhyme
1. Two words that end with the same sound.
2. The linguistic equivalent of a puzzle piece.

3. ....

Rhyme Scheme
1. A set pattern of rhymes that lasts for several lines of a song.
2. A way to organize and repeat the rhyme decisions you have made.

3. ....

Rhyming Couplet
1. A pair of lines in poetry that rhyme.
2. A literary device Shakespeare used to tell the audience a scene was over.

3. ....

Rhyming Dictionary
1. A book organized by words that rhyme with or sound similar to one another.
2. A helpful book that would probably also be a helpful website.

3. ....

Rhythm
1. The organization of time in songs, also known as "the beat."
2. The speed of a song.

3. ....

Song
1. A composition of words, ideas, and music.
2. A symphonic harmonic expression of one's deepest self.

3. ....

Staccato
1. Music where the notes are short and separate from each other.
2. Short. Notes. That. Do. Not. Blend. When. They. Are. Played.

3. ....

Symphony

1. A long musical composition comprised of many different instruments playing together.
2. A fancy concert at which men often fall asleep.

3. ....

Thesaurus

1. A book ("thesaurus" means "treasury") of words organized by similar meanings, to help you find just the right word choice.
2. A book of word choices that might make you sound way smarter than you feel.

3. ....

Verb

1. An action word.
2. A word that describes an activity.

3. ....

Verse

1. The story parts of a song divided up into structured chunks.
2. The boring part before the part that gets stuck in your head.

3. ....

Writer's Block

1. When you're trying so hard to come up with a good idea that you don't come up with any ideas.
2. A large piece of wood with drawers and a matching chair that sits in your bedroom or office.

3. ....

Extra Glossary Terms:

....

....

....

All Your New Tricks in One Place

Trick #1: *There is NO wrong way to write a song!*

Trick #2: *Save your ideas!*

Trick #3: *Write a song for a reason!*

Trick #4: *Ask WHY?!*

Trick #5: *Just start writing!*

Trick #6: *Set the scene!*

Trick #7: *The Verses are the story and the Chorus is how you feel about it.*

Trick #8: *Put your message in the Chorus!*

Trick #9: *The Bridge takes us somewhere else.*

Trick #10: *Bring me on your adventures!*

Trick #11: *Write what is true for You!*

Trick #12: *"Good writers borrow and great writers steal."*

Trick #13: *Write the thought, not the sentence!*

Trick #14: *Take the time and make it rhyme.*

Trick #15: *Set the (rhyme) scheme.*

Trick #16: *Check your rhymes out loud.*

Trick #17: *Harder doesn't make it better!*

Trick #18: *Sing it like it rhymes.*

Trick #19: *Invent a new word!*

Trick #20: *Similes are like diamonds and metaphors are gold!*

Trick #21: *Keep it simple.*

Trick #22: *Pick an instrument that sings to YOU!*

Trick #23: *Use your music to tell your story!*

Trick #24: *Do what's been done, only different!*

Trick #25: *Use your music as the feelings under your words.*

Trick #26: *Change the rhythm. Change the time.*

Trick #27: *You know best!*

Trick #28: ....

Trick #29: ....

Trick #30: ....

Trick #31: ....

Trick #32: ....

Trick #33: ....

Trick #34: ....

Trick #35: ....

Special Thank Yous!

Once you become a famous singer-songwriter, you will spend a ton of time thanking people who helped you achieve your success. Here is some space to make a list so you don't forget the amazing people in your life!

My Friends for hearing what wasn't finished:

My Family for loving my music even when it wasn't the best:

My Friend's Family for being so, so, so, so excited!

My Family's Friends for all that delicious food!

My Pet for his/her insight and thoughtful appreciation of life's simplicity:

About the Author

Danny Tieger can tie a bow tie, enjoys wearing silly hats, and hopes to live in a treehouse someday. His dad taught him how to write songs in middle school and he's been doing it ever since. Danny writes music for television and film with his band, Peter Panic. He's also performed for thousands of kids in hundreds of schools with the Story Pirates, an educational theater company. He's excited to teach you some of his favorite tricks for writing songs.

Danny lives in Brooklyn, New York, with his wife, Emily, and their rescue dog, Rocky.